Technology and Human Becoming

FACETS

Selected Titles in the Facets Series

Technology
and Human Becoming

Philip Hefner

Fortress Press
Minneapolis

This book originated as chapel talks at the 48th Annual Conference of the Institute on Religion in an Age of Science (28 July–4 August 2001, Star Island, New Hampshire).

Cover art: Chad Baker / Getty Images. Used by permission.

Frontispiece (p. vi): *La Mestiza Cosmica* by Lynn Randolph. Used by permission.

"Anecdote of the Jar" from *The Collected Poems of Wallace Stevens* by Wallace Stevens, copyright © 1954 by Wallace Stevens and renewed 1982 by Holly Stevens. Used by permission of Alfred A. Knopf, a division of Random House, Inc.

"Thyme Flowering among Rocks" from *Walking to Sleep: New Poems and Translations,* copyright © 1968 and renewed 1996 by Richard Wilbur, reprinted by permission of Harcourt, Inc.

ISBN 0-8006-3608-2

The paper used in this publication meets the minimum requirements of American National Standard for Information Sciences — Permanence of Paper for Printed Library Materials, ANSI Z329.48-1984.

Manufactured in the U.S.A.
07 06 05 04 03 1 2 3 4 5 6 7 8 9 10

In affection and gratitude
to the Institute on Religion in an Age of Science
and the Star Island Shoalers

Contents

Preface

Every July since 1954, the Institute on Religion in an Age of Science has convened a week-long annual conference on Star Island, one of the Isles of Shoals that sit in the boundary waters of Maine and New Hampshire. I have attended most of these conferences since 1977. The ferry trip, lasting an hour, eleven miles due east of Portsmouth, New Hampshire, is a journey from ordinary space and time into a world of virtual reality. The renowned anthropologist Victor Turner described it in terms that he made famous in his writings as a ritual of passage, a liminal journey that bears its participants across the threshold into a new state of existence, to enjoy a special kind of community. Since the point of this book is that technology is opening up a new world of meaning for human life today, it is fitting that it originated in that ritual journey to the islands.

I was privileged to serve as conference preacher for the 2001 conference, which convened under the theme, "Human Meaning in a Technological Culture." This book grows out of the talks that were delivered for six consecutive mornings in the stone chapel that sits atop the highest point of the island. Star Island has been inhabited continuously from the seventeenth century until today. This chapel was important for much of that time because the lantern in its belfry served as a beacon to sailing ships.

With very little alteration, the texts of those talks are presented in this little book. The attentive reader may imagine the sunny mornings in that craggy place, the sound of the ocean and the calls of the gulls intermingled with the words of the speaker. It was an appropriate place for reflection on the meaning of human existence in a technological age. In one sense, the rustic setting, which felt as if it were far removed from technological reality, provided a detached, quiet place for reflection. We were well aware, however, that in fact our week on the island would have been impossible without a panoply of technological aids that enabled us to have food, electricity, and water. Furthermore, we were never forgetful that the delicate ecosystem of people, island, and sea required foresight and carefulness as we used the enabling technology.

Most essential at Star Island, however, are the people, and I express here my gratitude to them for their indulgence and generosity. My thanks go to the planning committee members who, under the leadership of chairperson Willem Drees, invited me to be their daily speaker. Thanks and admiration go also to the listeners in the chapel—their encouragement, provocative conversation, and helpful suggestions afterwards were as important as the technology that brought us together and sustained us for that week.

1

Locating the Spiritual Journey

Two images to spark reflection on technology.

The first:
A man standing in the hills of Tennessee, reflecting on the system of dams and power stations that made up the Tennessee Valley Authority (TVA).

> I placed a jar in Tennessee.
> And round it was, upon a hill.
> It made the slovenly wilderness
> Surround that hill.
>
> The wilderness rose up to it,
> And sprawled around, no longer wild.
> The jar was round upon the ground
> And tall and of a port in air.
> It took dominion everywhere.

The jar was gray and bare.
It did not give of bird or bush,
Like nothing else in Tennessee.[1]

The second:
A man standing in the Nevada desert,
looking at the place where the first atomic
bomb was exploded, and that same man
making his way through, inside, a nearly
completed cyclotron in Berkeley in the
early 1950s. I read from his written record
of what went through his mind at those
two places related to nuclear energy.

By the liberation of atomic energy on a
massive scale, and for the first time,
humans have not only changed the face
of the earth; they have by the very act
set in motion at the heart of their being
a long chain of reactions which, in the
brief flash of an explosion of matter, has
made of them, virtually at least, a new
being hitherto unknown to themselves.[2]

. . . the forming of a completely new
psychic reality whose nature is as yet
unexplored.[3]

For hardly had I become sensitive to the
"odor" of the ultra-human given off by

the huge atomic turbines I was looking at,
than I suddenly recognized in it the ema-
nations which surround all the other
great machines that for the last half-
century have been continually growing
up in every quarter, under our eyes, like
so many gigantic trees: Electronic microscopes and gigantic telescopes, rockets
with inter-planetary potentialities, computers (the vitalisation of matter by the
creation of supermolecules), the remodel-
ing of the human organism by means of
hormones, control of heredity and sex by
the manipulation of genes and chromo-
somes, the readjustment and internal liberation of our souls by psycho-analysis.[4]

At all these nodal points, the same chain
process can surely be clearly recognized:
people at first sucked up by, made pris-
oner by, the object of their efforts and
then finally transformed.[5]

Two symbols of technology, the jar and
the man-inside-the-cyclotron. The jar is
the enemy of nature—"it did not give of
bird or bush"—the very opposite of nature,
the despoiler of nature, and hence the
enemy of every human, as well. The

cyclotron and the release of atomic energy are occasions for the transformation of nature, and that includes most dramatically the transformation of us, human persons; a pivotal point in the process of making ourselves into new beings.

In case you are wondering, the image of the jar was given to us by the poet Wallace Stevens in his poem, "Anecdote of the Jar." Teilhard de Chardin, the French Jesuit priest and paleontologist, reflected on the cyclotron and the atomic bomb.

These two images could stand before us as two clearly opposed ways of interpreting technology, two perspectives that exist at opposite ends of a spectrum. Fear, disgust, repudiation at one end, exultation and celebration at the other. In these chapters, however, I am not presenting these images as contradictory perspectives on technology. Rather, I propose that they are stations on the journey of human becoming. They do designate differing points of view through which we observe technology "out there." They are also ways of expressing the changing process of how we understand ourselves "in here," how we are becoming human and our sense of technology's part in that process.

In line with this approach, I do not view these reflections as a resource for a course entitled "Technology 101" so much as for a course entitled "Human Nature 101," with special attention to the technological and religious dimensions of human nature. I do not want to exaggerate this distinction because it is something we must wrestle with if we are to understand ourselves fully. Clarity that comes too easily is the enemy of deeper understanding.

We must make the struggle to understand how the two courses are related if we are to grasp the deepest significance of technology, if we are to perceive its deepest meaning. Human becoming is a deeply spiritual and religious process. I do not say "becoming human," because that sounds as if being human is a final destination, and if we get on the right train, we will finally reach the station called "being human." "Human becoming" expresses the idea that we are *always in process*, we are a becoming, and being human means that the journey is the reality—there may well be no *final* destination. This journey is a religious reality, a journey of the spirit, and if technology is a part of it, then technology is also a religious and spiritual reality.

In these six chapters, I will focus on these questions: What is technology's place in the processes of our becoming, that is, within our very human nature? What is the spiritual, religious meaning of technology?

Since Stevens's image of the jar is important for what it says about our human nature, it has religious meaning. Dams that harness water flow, power stations that transform water force into electricity, pylons and wires that transmit that electricity—all these are instruments of human convenience. They are technological artifice that portrays our fundamental difference from and antithesis to nature. If we need cheap electricity, and lots of it, and if this technology is the way we get it, we demonstrate that we are not only dependent on unnatural technology, we are aliens within nature's realm. We take the wild out of wilderness—Stevens says—we make nature slovenly, we exercise gray and bare dominion. What more expressive image than that of the jar? Mother put up preserves and pickles in those Mason jars—when they were made of glass. Now, whether glass or plastic, everything from jelly to green catsup to toilet bowl cleaner comes in those jars. The jar is the symbol of what humans do with technology. And it becomes a symbol of the humans who do it with technology.

As a symbol of humans—of us—in our process of becoming, the jar says something about our spirituality. In fact, it places us before a fork in the road, a choice that will determine how our spiritual journey proceeds. If we affirm technology, which the jar symbolizes, then we believe that our spiritual task, our religious calling, is to dominate and manipulate the natural world around us. The poet interprets this as perversity; he believes that our spiritual calling is to destroy the technology and support nature.

Whatever choice we make at this fork, the issue is how we relate to the natural environment. The religious or spiritual issue is whether we develop technology, which is destructive, or go another way—against technology. The imagery definitely begins with warfare.

Stevens's anecdote portrays the dualism for which our Western traditions are so notorious. Humans against nature, culture against nature, technology, the fruit of human culture, against nature. Humans and their technological culture are "like nothing else in Tennessee." This is who we are, in Stevens's time and today. We still hear talk of our medical practice as "medicine against nature." We advertise our NASA space program as "the conquest of space." We say that efforts to reverse global warming are *against* our American economy. This is also warfare imagery. And religious imagery: the medical and space conquests are often invested with religious meaning and religious sanction. So is the American economy. Some, like Wallace Stevens, would make global warming a matter of religion, as well.

We can say that the jar expresses an inadequate view of nature. I want to say that, whether adequate or inadequate, it is a view of *human* nature. And as a view of human nature, it has religious implications, religious depth. It puts us in the middle of a battlefield and asks us to choose sides as to how culture, technology, and nature will be related. This is its spiritual challenge.

Whereas it is possible to look at Stevens's jar as an image of the nature *external* to us, Teilhard gives us an unmistakable image of *internality* and what it means to become human. However one assesses the atom bomb and nuclear energy—as well as microscopes, telescopes, rockets, computers, genetic engineering of all sorts—Teilhard images them as internal to us and our becoming. For him the question can never be first of all "what are we *doing* with our technology?" but it must be "what are we *becoming* with our technology?" The jar is an image of technology as "outsideness," whereas Teilhard is *inside* the cyclotron.

That "inside" perspective reveals that we are a facet of earth's evolution, our releasing the energy of the atom through technological interventions is part of a physical, biological, and psychic process of evolution itself. So he can write that the atomic test in Nevada reveals that this event of human technology is accomplished by the energy of the universe, an awakening of the "slumbering energies of matter and thought." He goes on:

> So that today there exists in each of us a person whose mind has been opened to the meaning, the responsibility and the aspirations of our cosmic function in the universe; a person, that is to say, who whether we like it or not has been transformed into another person, in our very depths.[6]

Teilhard frames the religious-spiritual issue differently from Stevens. Technology is not located in a battlefield, but rather in a process of evolutionary becoming. Technology belongs to our becoming, it belongs to nature's becoming, and to the becoming of the universe. Technology is energy, the energy of an awakening and growing cosmos. What a different way of interpreting the spiritual meaning of technology and its place in human life!

With this image, we understand that human becoming is nature's becoming, the becoming of the cosmos. If that event in the Nevada desert marked an innovation, it was like the innovation that happens when a child becomes a teenager, or when a young adult becomes middle-aged. As marvelous as the new event is, it is not so much an innovation as an unfolding, a phase of growth. At least, that is Teilhard's view.

We can pose the question whether the image of the jar is more or less adequate than the image of Teilhard inside the cyclotron. Indeed, we must raise that question. We might ask, as well, whether the one image belongs to an earlier phase of our becoming, say the phase of adolescence, whereas the other belongs to our adulthood. Or, again, we might ask whether the adolescent is not always within the adult, so that both the jar and the man-in-the-cyclotron describe our becoming as human persons.

These issues raise many questions. Questions about how technology works, what it is supposed to accomplish, what its consequences are, whether its use is ethically permissible, whether it is environment-friendly or human-friendly. These are important and necessary questions. These are the questions we need to answer if we expect to get a passing grade in Technology 101. But there is another set of questions that I want to raise, the questions *about us*. The questions about human becoming. These are the questions pertinent to another course, Human Nature 101.

As we approach this second exam, we are impressed how technology is *rearranging* our world, rearranging our views of human nature, rearranging the religious question. I said earlier that unless we know how to relate technology and human nature, we will not grasp the meaning of technology, and we will not grasp the religious issues posed by technology. I said that I am attempting to locate our spiritual journey. Now I will say that its location is in technology.

Everything we think about religion, everything we think is *spiritual*, is rearranged by technology. If spirituality means something about creation to you, if it means sin and forgiveness, if it means overcoming adversity, if it means love, if it means personal fulfillment, if it means hope—all of these must be reconceived and reexperienced in the medium of technology. The jar is technologized sin, the cyclotron is technologized hope and spiritual fulfillment. At least for Stevens and Teilhard. How is it for you?

2

The Movement from Techno-World to Techno-Self: The Question of Alienation and Reconciliation

The jar in Tennessee. Is it an image of the dams, power stations, and delivery systems for electricity and flood control? Or is it an image of the humans who designed, built, authorized, paid for, and used them? Is the jar an image of the technology "out there"—as palpably "out there" as the mountains, forests, rivers, and dams of Tennessee? Or is it about you and me, the people who put it there in Tennessee? Is it about the outside techno-world? Or about the inside techno-self: techno-me and techno-you?

If you have seen the Stanley Kubrick / Steven Spielberg movie, *A.I. Artificial Intelligence* (2001), you recall the scene of the Flesh Fair, presided over by Lord Johnson-Johnson. David, the robot boy or "mecha" (for "mechanical"), who has been programmed to love his foster mother, is abandoned, rounded up, and taken to an arena full of jeering onlookers. The scene is reminiscent of a nighttime demolition derby under floodlights combined with the riot in which Chicago police attacked and clubbed the protesters at the 1968 Democratic Convention. David is a target for the most brutal demolition, with Lord Johnson-Johnson egging on the attackers, with his blow-by-blow account from center stage. The crime the mechas have committed, he growls, is to resemble human beings. In that very act of verisimilitude, the robots ridicule and degrade human persons.

If you reacted as I did, your heart spontaneously went out to the robot-boy, David, and you projected your anger directly upon the humans who were crying for David's "blood." In this situation, *New York Times* reviewer A. O. Scott asks, "If we side with David and his mechanical brethren against their human oppressors, are we affirming our humanity or have we been irrevocably alienated from it?"[1] This is another instance of the techno-world / techno-self question. If technology is essentially "out there" and "other" from us, then it makes no sense to empathize with David; it is absurd to do so. On the other hand, if there is any sense whatsoever in which David is us, then only insensitivity would be indifferent to his fate at the Flesh Fair.

A third image that portrays the duality between outside techno-world and inside techno-self: Two years ago, I underwent a colonoscopy with no sedation. I watched the proceedings on the television monitor as avidly as I used to watch the Chicago Bulls win their string of NBA championships. What was I watching? An external image made possible through external technological means? It reminded me of the movie *Mysterious Voyage,* in which a miniaturized medical team sails through the circulatory system of a desperately ill man. Or was it my own self I was watching? To this day, whenever I think of my own insides, I image them on that screen and think of that lighted probe negotiating the twists and turns of my body.

The social philosopher Donna Haraway deals at length with the phenomenon of the colonoscopy. She cites the painting by Lynn Randolph, *Immeasurable Results.* In this painting, the recumbent body of a draped woman is about to enter a Magnetic Resonance Imaging (MRI) device. On the wall above the slab on which the woman lies is a framed picture. Let me present Haraway's description of this painting-within-a-painting that artist Randolph presents to us:

> a pocketwatch without clock hands, armed instead with crab claws, whose nightmare timekeeping is outside mechanical chronology; a red demon hammering at the skull, echoing the pounding heard by the woman inside the MRI machine, punctuating the staccato bits of information emitted from the brain-machine interface; a day-of-the-dead Mexican skeleton poised with a spear to announce the impending death lurking in the traitorous flesh; an alligator-predator; and, in the center of this ring of surrealist beings, the technical, medical frontal section, cut without knives, through the brain, sinus cavities, and throat. All of these images—certainly including the bloodless optical slice of the woman's head and neck—are intensely personal. The moment of reading and scanning, of being read and being scanned, is the moment of vulnerability.[2]

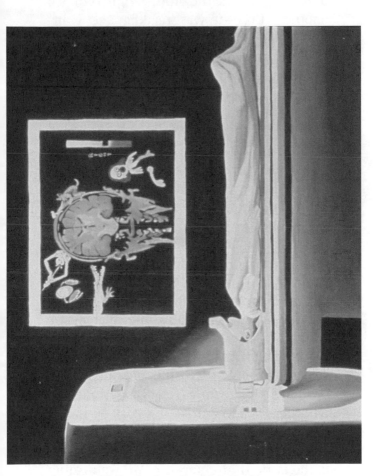

Immeasurable Results, Lynn Randolph. Used by permission.

(As I watched my colonoscopy, I held my breath every time the probing light rounded another curve—it was reading and scanning, being read and being scanned, a moment of vulnerability.)

Haraway's point is that the boundary between technology and human self has been utterly erased in this experience with the MRI; it is portrayed in the Randolph painting and in its double entendre title—*Immeasurable Results*. The painting depicts what we might call "technological self-fashioning."[3]

The MRI device, the technical rendering of the woman's physiology, in the form that her doctors will receive it, the fear of death symbolized by the Mexican figure with the spear, the nonexistence of time for her, symbolized by the surrealistic watch, and her actual body, entering the MRI—all of these are equally her personal self. All are equally inside and outside her selfhood. Her techno-world has coalesced with her techno-self.

When we juxtapose the image of the jar with that of the woman in the MRI, what is the issue that emerges? Are we dealing with a chronological record here? The Tennessee jar might seem to be an almost quaint image of externality. After all, Stevens's world had few, if any colonoscopies, no MRI's, no ideas of robot boys who could love their mothers and be trashed by rednecks. The distance between the two sets of images is the distance our technological development has traversed in seventy years.

Or are we dealing not with chronology but with the dynamics of the self and the psyche? Have Steven Spielberg and Lynn Randolph recounted the trajectory of human becoming that everyone of us, in fact, must say is our own journey? It is a journey of understanding technology, and it is also a journey of our own personal becoming. It is not really a chronological record we are dealing with here at all. I suggested before that the earlier phases of human development coexist in the later phases. The infant is always present in the adolescent, and the adolescent in turn is always present in the adult. Stevens's jar is just as much a symbol of who we are as Randolph's woman in the MRI. The outside of technology is as inside us as the inside is outside. When I watched my colonoscopy, I lost all sense of the difference between inside and outside.

Perhaps my images are too dramatic, too unusual, to convey the experience of us all. We should not make technology too dramatic. It should appear ordinary, even trivial, as well, because most of our daily life is spelled out in the ordinary and the trivial. There are countless ordinary ways in which we have acted out the ritual of Randolph's painting—entering into technology and permitting technology to enter into us. The ordinariness of eyeglasses is a vessel of the spirit for those of us who could not read or write without them. The pharmacological products of technology enter into us in the most intimate way—we ingest them and they become integral to our body and mind. High blood pressure, diabetes, depression—just to name a few— would destroy our selfhood if not for our ingesting certain fruits of technology. Implants and artificial parts—cardiac, orthodontal, optical, cochlear, hips and knees—very quickly extinguish the boundaries between technological outside and inside as they make life possible and fuller. Many of us are now so intimately connected to our computers that our creativity—whether it is writing or graphic art, or interpersonal communication, mathematical modeling, or other research procedures—is integrated with the machine, and the computer scarcely qualifies as an entity that exists "outside" our spirits.

These technological mergers with our bodies and spirits are so ordinary that technical support for our computers, medical care, and prescription subsidies very nearly become as basic as food, clothing, and housing in a society like ours. They are no longer phenomena that occur in our culture, but they are rather dimensions of our culture.

I said earlier that the journey of our becoming is religious, a spiritual, reality, because that journey takes us to the depths of our search for identity and the meaning of our lives. I also suggested that our spiritual reality becomes technologized. "Technologized" is not a felicitous term; it is hard, with an unpretty sound. I use it intentionally, because it is jarring, and that very quality safeguards it from being banal. It grabs our attention.

We are getting more specific about human becoming. We are talking about the formation of our *self*, our self-image, our image of who we are. Whether it is Lynn Randolph's woman in the MRI or our taking prescription drugs for depression or high blood pressure, it is the image of our self that is at issue. There is scarcely anything in life that we consider more precious, more spiritually charged, than our selfhood and its formation. Now we are talking about this selfhood as *technologized*. What happens now? How do we respond to the technologization of what is most precious to us personally?

We must introduce the idea of alienation. The journey of personal formation that is marked by techno-world and techno-self, outside and inside, is never uneventful. It is always marked also by alienation and the quest for reconciliation. Today, the dominant responses to technology in our society include ambivalence, fear, and repugnance. Popular culture expresses this clearly, in movies, journalism, and grass-roots social movements— from Charlie Chaplin's *Modern Times* to *Gattaca,* and the popular protests against genetically altered foods and nuclear power. While ambivalence is the rule on some issues of technology, like stem cell research, fear and dread govern responses to others, like genetically altered foods and cloning. Often these responses are contradictory, since even if we fear technology, we continue to require technological assistance throughout our daily lives. We take our pills in the morning, put on our glasses, check our e-mail for instructions, and drive our technically sophisticated cars to a rally protesting genetic interventions in plant and human organisms.

These responses permeate religion. Christians and Muslims have a difficult time understanding *Gattaca* as a movie about God's creation. Buddhists have equal difficulty understanding that their meditative practices can be at home in the techno-world. I am generalizing, of course, but the exceptions do prove the rule.

Alienation is the proper word for our attitudes toward the journey from techno-world to techno-self. It would be strange if no one were offended by my references to my colonoscopy. Lynn Randolph's painting is not a pleasant one; if we placed a life-size copy of it in a church, it would seem out of place, I am sure, to some of us.

The alienation runs very deep in our culture. That is why we so commonly give voice to the dualisms of people versus nature, culture versus nature, technology versus people and nature. It is one thing to feel the alienation creep within us as we read Stevens's poem about the jar; we also project that alienation outward. We are doing that with some regularity today, in regard to drilling for oil in the Arctic National Wildlife Refuge (ANWR) or in national parks or genetically altered foods. If the Tennessee Valley Authority (TVA) were proposing nuclear power plants, we would bring out Stevens's poem as if it were written today. All of these technological projects awaken alienation, but we project that alienation outward. If we favor drilling in ANWR, we project it against those environmental "pinheads." If we oppose it, we talk about "those profit-hungry oil companies."

It is something else again, and something even more poignant and potentially destructive, when we feel that alienation turning against our very selves. When it is only technology and its products that enables us to have children, or to maintain our lives, or to sustain the standard of living without which we would consider life not worth living, the technology from which we are alienated is thoroughly integrated into our being. A Chicago talk-show host derided the movie *A.I.* and those who said they cared about David. "How could you care about him?" she cried out, "You knew he was only a robot." That is the voice of alienation, because she was effectively denying how much of David is embodied in herself. Even if we are not robots, we *are* cyborgs, and the intelligence of the robot is our intelligence, it is modeled after ours.

Our attitudes toward technology are a very sensitive and reliable litmus test of our alienation from contemporary life. Alienation is serious, because it is a malignancy, it destroys life, whether slowly or quickly. Alienation raises the question of reconciliation. Spielberg brilliantly tells the story of the human need for robots who can love humans. In this respect, David embodies reconciliation. His human designers could not, however, produce a human foster father, foster brother, or even a foster mother, who could love a robot in return. So, the very existence of reconciliation in the designer's robot threw a strong spotlight on the alienation that yet remained in the hearts of the humans who created David and desired him.

The journey from techno-world to techno-self is a fact of our history. Perhaps it was inevitable. As a process of human becoming, it reveals our alienation from the world we live in, the world we have in part made. At the same time, it promises a reconciliation of great proportions, a reconciliation of the kind that Teilhard celebrated, when he spoke of technology as the occasion for our transformation into beings of a new order.

What degree of reconciliation would it take for robot-boy David's foster mother to love him? At the end of the movie, as a clone, she does in fact say, "I love you." What does it take for Randolph's woman-in-the-MRI to internalize the self that is being scanned and read by the machine? The self that is imaged by the optical slice of her head and neck? Of course, Randolph's painting is about this process of internalization, so it is actually a painting of the woman's becoming, her becoming a new person. What does it take for any of us to respond receptively to technology as the process of our own becoming new persons?

Alienation and reconciliation are at the heart of religion. Judaism focuses on God's acts of reconciliation toward Israel—that is what the Covenant is about.

The enormous amount of reflection and writing Jews have devoted to the Law has to do with the effort to be reconciled, to overcome the alienation within Israel and within each individual person, so that personal and communal life can conform in obedience to the reconciliation wrought by Yahweh. Christians believe that we are created without alienation, that it is a result of sin, and that in Jesus, God reconciles us to God's self, to the creation, to other persons, and to ourselves. In the process, God became human, became incarnated in human nature.

If our self is techno-self, what is added to our understanding of alienation and reconciliation? How does that techno-self impact our religious traditions? How, for example, for Christians, does God become flesh when that flesh is techno-flesh? What would reconciliation look like, if it was to be a true reconciliation for techno-world and techno-self? Think about that.

3

Seeing Ourselves
in the Techno-Mirror

"Mirror, mirror, on the wall, tell me. . . ." Tell me who I am. Imagine for a moment that technology can be that mirror.

"Does technology tell us what we want to do, our desires for accomplishing things? Or does it tell us who we are and what we wish to be? I hope that at this point you agree that these questions are quite at the center of any consideration of technology. These questions—what we want to do and who we are—are inseparable. In some ways, they are the same question viewed from different angles. Both of them show up in the techno-mirror.

How did this happen, that technology became a mirror?

Let us begin with Alan Turing, an Englishman who was born in 1912 (just before World War I), was honored for his inventions that helped to win World War II, and died in the midst of the Cold War in 1954. He was a key figure in the development of information technology, computers, what he called, "thinking machines." He suggested the famous "Turing test," by which he meant a kind of guessing game. "If a computer, on the basis of its written replies to questions, could not be distinguished from a human respondent, then 'fair play' would oblige one to say that it must be 'thinking.'"[1]

Turing was interested in machines for their own sake, for the ability to resolve problems of thought, specifically problems of mathematics and the philosophy of mathematics as posed by thinkers such as Hilbert and Goedel. In order to resolve such problems, machines would have to imitate human thinking, including the ability to learn, teach, search, and make decisions.[2] Thus, Turing placed the mirror at the center of his computer technology—the computer is a reflection of human thinking.

Turing rejected the notion that there is a force or "mind" behind the brain that is responsible for what the brain does. Rather, what the brain *does* is all there is.[3]

Turing made certain basic decisions that guided his brilliant innovative work. First, it is not the biology or the physics of the brain that is critical for what it does, but rather the *logical structure of its activities*. Therefore, those activities can be represented in any medium that replicates that structure of logic, including machines.[4]

Second, it is thinking that is the critical characteristic. Imagine a different guessing game, Turing suggests, in which a questioner would have to decide, on the basis of written replies, which of two persons was a man and a woman. The man would be trying to deceive the questioner, while the woman tried equally to respond convincingly as to who she was. If the man succeeded in convincing the questioner that he was a woman, it would prove nothing, because gender is not a matter of imitation. Thinking is, however. This is how he constructed his mirror, and that plays a role in determining what the mirror will reflect back to us.

Turing wanted his technology to resolve classic thought problems. The British government wanted that technology to crack German codes during the World War II, while the United States government also wanted such technology to replace human workers in the postal system. The one desire is purely intellectual, the other is practical. Both assume that technology should imitate human beings, upon the further assumption that thinking is the critical human trait. The result has been three-quarters of a century discussion of how humans think and how that thinking can be replicated in a nonbiological medium. Consider the billions of dollars that have been invested in this technology and the thousands of our most brilliant thinkers and inventors who have given their lives to developing it. The mirror is neither small nor unpretentious nor inexpensive.

Turing and his colleagues and their descendants have created a significant mirror of ourselves. What we want and who we are coalesce in this mirror. Whether we think this mirror is adequate or not is another question.

In the Kubrick / Spielberg movie *A.I. Artificial Intelligence* we see a different line of Turing's descendants. This technology for producing robots accepts the assumption that imitating human behavior is fundamental, and it works equally on the hypothesis that humans are what humans do. But thinking is not the critical mark of being human—*loving* is. Robot- boy David is unique, or at least the first of a unique line of robots, because he can be programmed to be imprinted and to love forever the person who imprints upon him. When his foster mother Monica performs the imprinting ritual, David's total existence is driven by his love for her, throughout the two-thousand-year time-span that the movie covers. Turing and Kubrick-Spielberg agree that the technological robot must be able to learn and make decisions, and that biology is not essential for this hallmark of human behavior, love. They disagree sharply on what they want to do and on what is most important about humans. David is designed to meet the human need for love. Joe, a robot gigolo who approximates David's level of achievement, also exists for serving that need. Kubrick and Spielberg, working on Turing's principles, have created a mirror that reflects images quite different from Turing's.

Think for a moment how the mirror presented by *A.I.* is both similar to Turing's and also different. Note the responses that the two robots elicit from humans. Turing asks us whether we can think as well as the computer—beat Big Blue at chess or resolve a mathematical problem too complex for ordinary minds. Or, perhaps, simply to accept the usefulness of speedy calculations. David and Gigolo Joe bid us to respond with love, whether parental or sexual. The negative responses to these forms of computer technology are equally revealing in the mirror. David and Joe elicit fear, hatred, and savagery. David's foster parents and brother fear him (and, to an extent, hate him), leading them to abandon him to the Flesh Fair. One of Joe's clients is afraid to have sex with him, even though she engaged his services. Replicating our emotions seems to affect us at a different level than replicating our thinking processes. Or should we say that thinking with our hearts represents a different dimension of our being than thinking with our intellects. Some would say that gender is critical here: men focus on chess and math, while women are sensitive to the importance of love and relationships. Since all of this computer technology has been developed by groups that are predominantly male, however, one wonders whether the gender issue is not more complex than this. The gender issue is certainly there, but in what form?

Let us be specific: if technology is the mirror, mirror, on the wall, what are the main images it reflects back to us as we peer into it? I call attention to four such images.

1. The techno-mirror shows us that we want tools to do things for us, and it shows us what we want done. We want these things for our survival and also for our pleasure.

We want tools that will cure our diseases, correct our defects, and make us more beautiful.

We want tools that will extract the useful products that are embedded in the earth and sea and atmosphere.

We want to live complex lives, accomplish complex goals, and we want the tools that will make that possible—cars, planes, phones, fax machines, computers, and intellectual agents. We invest all of these with urgency; we consider them to be *basic needs*. Curing disease and extracting resources have become quasi-religious activities. While we do not yet pray for better oil rigs or cell phones, we pray regularly for new cures and good doctors.

2. The techno-mirror shows us that we are finite, frail, and mortal.

Technology is about being finite and mortal. We create technology in order to compensate for our finitude. That could almost serve as a definition of what tools are—devices for compensating for human finitude.

Since technology can outlive us, be stronger than we are, more accurate, and faster, the very existence of our technology reminds us of our finitude and mortality. Frank J. Tipler theorizes about computer technology in a book entitled, *The Physics of Immortality.*[5] Simply by being there, technology of all kinds expresses the truth that we need technical assistance in order to become who and what we want to be, because our finitude does not carry us as far as we want to go.

In the classic Ridley Scott film *Blade Runner* (1982), we see this clearly. Robots, known as "replicants," are designed and built in order to live and work in extraterrestrial environments that are hostile to human beings. Since those robots must be designed to be stronger than their creators, and at the high end of human intelligence, they constitute a potential threat to humans. Therefore, they are programmed to self-destruct after a few years. Since the assumption here, in contrast to Turing and Kubrick-Spielberg, is that human intelligence is necessarily biological, the robots are genetically engineered. Consequently, the entire movie is about dying. The replicants become aware of their programmed mortality and rebel. The human creators lack the know-how to reverse the programmed self-destruction. The movie focuses on two replicants: one, Roy, who, after his rebellion, acknowledges his death and dies with grace and nobility in the climactic finish. The other, Rachel, who has been programmed with a high-level emotionality, becomes romantically involved with the terminator of replicants, Rick Deckard, played by Harrison Ford. The romance is thwarted by her self-destruct programming.[6]

The robot boy in *A.I.* desires to be human, only to discover that being human means to be mortal, and when he finally fulfills his dream to be a real human boy, he dies. *A.I.,* in a sense, is also about dying.

A good deal of our technology seems to be a denial of death and an attempt to escape it. Think of genetic engineering and genetic medicine, extraterrestrial exploration and colonization: Genetic engineering and medicine enable us to live longer. Extraterrestrial exploration and colonization enable our species to escape the destruction of planet earth when the sun's evolution brings it to the Red Giant phase, in which it will consume the earth.

In its engagement with finitude and death, technology becomes almost explicitly religious. Paul Tillich has said that religion focuses on what we care about most, what we are dependent on. This is his concept of *ultimate concern.*[7] He also said that the mark of a theological issue is that it deals with what makes for our being or not-being. The struggle with finitude and death meets all these criteria: it is a matter of religion and raises theological questions. Since it is a medium for these concerns and questions, technology is both religious and theological. Indeed, technology may be more religiously gripping than a sacred liturgy and more theologically urgent than a sacred dogma.

The *Blade Runner* replicant's rebellion against death and his murder of the human designer is a religious response—lashing out at God, cursing God. The replicant's acceptance of death is also a religious response, even though it is not clear whether it marks a peaceful, confident coming to terms with death, or futility and resignation.

Ernest Becker chronicled our culture's denial of death.[8] He said it is a driving force in American life. The movie *Gattaca* articulates Becker's point: genetically engineered perfect babies, educational and job opportunities available only to those genetically superior men and women. All the more interesting that in so many of these movies—*A.I., Blade Runner, Gattaca,*—the victory goes to the mortals and the defectives. *Gattaca* is an especially vivid example: Two brothers are in competition—one perfectly engineered, the other, a defective "love child" conceived during his parents' backseat passion. The defective brother successfully hides his genetic identity and finally surpasses his brother when he saves him from drowning and is later selected to be an astronaut. It is as if these movies are repudiating denial and finding deeper value in finitude and mortality. There is at least one world religion that also suggests that a man who was defeated and executed on a cross turned out, finally, to be the victor. Or perhaps these movies are a sturdy witness to the belief that mortal, finite creatures have intrinsic worth of their own. In my Lutheran tradition, we call this Justification by Grace or, as it is known more technically, "It's okay to be mortal."

3. We see in the techno-mirror that we create technology in order to bring alternative worlds into being, worlds that differ from the actual worlds in which we live.

We insist on creating a virtual reality to counterbalance the reality that is given to us. The genetic technology that may well be a denial of our mortality can also be a means to create an alternative state of life. In my next chapter, I reflect more on the close relationship between behaviors of denial and behaviors that create new, alternative worlds. The ability to create alternative worlds underscores Teilhard's comments on technology as "supercreative." We can rearrange matter, we can put the pieces of nature's jigsaw puzzle together in unusual ways, in order to create new combinations and realities. We are not at all reluctant to say that these new realities are religiously charged.

4. *Finally, we see in the mirror that although we are busy creating new realities, we do not know why we create or according to what values—so we have to discover the reasons and the values.*

The techno-mirror reveals to us that we do not know with certainty the answers to questions of "Why do we do this?" and "Is it a good thing to do?" The mirror shows us, further, that as human creators, we do not even agree on the possible answers to these questions:

- Pro-life / pro-choice?
- Cloning?
- What should guide our genetic engineering of humans? What models of personhood come into play?
- Should we genetically engineer other creatures and plants? What does such engineering say about our attitude toward the rest of nature?

These questions take us to yet a deeper level of our journey of human becoming—we came to the realization in our first reflections that our journey is unavoidably technological; we gave attention to how technology shapes our self-image. Now we see that technology intensifies the perennial ambiguities of our human journey, because it poses the issues of finitude and death, of the purposes of the journey and its morality—the right and wrong of the journey. The answers to these questions are not given to us, we must discover them.

Now we come to the most perplexing questions of all, reflected in the techno-mirror: Do the virtual selves that we create in our technology help us to understand who we are, bring us closer to knowing ourselves? Or do they distract us, raising even more difficult questions of what it means to be human? Does it really help to see our images in Turing machines? Or in genetically modified embryos? Should we take the techno-mirror from the wall and throw it to the ground? Does breaking the mirror actually bring bad consequences? Or would it be better to break it?

The techno-mirror drawn by Teilhard reflects images of excitement, adventure, cosmic significance, liberation. The techno-mirrors drawn by Kubrick and Spielberg in *A.I.* and by Ridley Scott in *Blade Runner* do reflect beauty, but also weakness, ignorance, greed, savagery, and death.

Techno-mirror on the wall—tell me, what do you see? Who is the "me" that you reflect?

4

The Essence:
To Be Free and Free to Imagine

In his reflections on the atom bomb, Teilhard writes,

> The fact of the release of nuclear energy, overwhelming and intoxicating though it was, began to seem less tremendous. Was it not simply the first act, even a mere prelude, in a series of fantastic events which, having afforded us access to the heart of the atom, would lead us on to overthrow, one by one, the many other strongholds which science is already besieging? Is not every kind of effect produced by a suitable arrangement of matter? And have we not reason to hope that in the end we shall be able to arrange every kind of matter, following the results we have obtained in the nuclear field?[1]

> In exploding the atom we took our first bite at the fruit of the great discovery, and this was enough for a taste to enter our mouths that can never be washed away: the taste for super-creativeness.[2]

Technology as the rearranging of matter, the taste for supercreativeness. What is the significance of this supercreativeness? What is it *about*? There is a clue, once again, in the movie *A.I.,* when one of the forty-first century robots speaks about humans. By this time, humans have gone the way of the dinosaur, and robots have surpassed them in most respects. Twentieth-century robot-boy David has been in hibernation for two millennia, and when he is awakened he discovers that he is instantly a "treasure," because he is the only robot in existence who had direct contact with humans. What is so important about humans? David is told: The greatest gift of humans is that they wish for things that do not exist. *Only humans can believe in what is not actual.*

I have said technology is about our being finite, frail, and mortal. Technology is also about being free and imagining things and conditions that never were, things that do not exist, and conditions that can be different. Teilhard was wrong about one thing; this did not happen only with the atomic age. The first stone tool was the product of the imagination, of picturing the nonexistent into existence, the skinning of a mammoth or the scaling of a fish. Genetic engineering, whether for reasons of therapy, improvement, or personal preference, rests on our imagining that which does not actually exist. The same can be said of computer technology. "Virtual" reality is reality conditioned by our dreaming of what is not yet actual but might become so. When it is not possible or not feasible to rearrange actual walls and cities, we move virtual objects by replicating perceptions that correspond to what we imagine. I'll go out on a limb and say that technology is entirely the product of our imagination, and what we want it to be is likewise conditioned by imagination and by our free decisions to imagine what we want done and the tools for getting it done. It may be as solid as a big yellow bulldozer, as massive as a cyclotron, or as fragile as a computer or laser knife, but its foundations are laid in the human imagination.

In addition, I said that technology seems to be carried out as a strategy for denying our mortality and death. It is also a means for surpassing finitude and death, in that imagining what is not but might be is a form of transcendence within our mind and spirit. The line between denial and surpassing or transcending is not an easy one to see. Perhaps there is no line. Perhaps denying and transcending are two sides of the same coin. Perhaps denying what is, is the presupposition for transcending it.

When we consider how fundamental imagination is to technology and to human life, we also broaden our idea of technology. In his series of "fantastic events" of which the atom bomb is but the first, Teilhard listed chemistry, genetics, and psychotherapy. He is not the only one who has interpreted psychotherapy as a kind of technology. It certainly rests on the foundation of human imagination, in its conceptualizing what the self is, as well as in its ideas of what the self can become. We might even speak of religion as a technology. Some anthropologists say that practices using alcohol and hallucinogenic drugs originated within religion. Their purpose may have been to actualize imaginary states of mind and spirit that we believe are desirable or even necessary for our transcendence. Dreams and rituals fall in this category as well. Rituals of passage and puberty aim to make idealized states as real as actual ones.

Examples of ritual virtual reality can be taken from every religion. I think of the rites of early Christian initiation. For forty days prior to Easter, a group of persons has undergone intensive instruction, or catechesis. On Easter eve, late at night, they undergo their rite of initiation, coinciding with the remembrance of the night when Jesus made his transition from the death of the grave to new life in the resurrection. The initiates strip off their clothes and are plunged into the water of the baptismal pool. When they emerge, they are given identical white robes, and they participate in their first Holy Communion, eating the bread and drinking the wine that symbolize unity with Jesus and with the community of his followers. Note what alternative reality is being imagined and created: (1) each initiate sees the others stripped; a bond of common humanity is thereby formed, distinctions of class and status are leveled away; (2) all are washed, purified in the same baptismal bath; (3) all now dress in identical pure white robes; and (4) all share the sacrament of unity with Jesus and their fellow Christians. This is their new world—they are now brothers and sisters, stripped of their old garb and given identical new clothes; they are *new* people cleansed in the same water; their primary reference group is now the community of Christians. Is this new world actual or virtual? Is it real? Is it a dominant feature of their identity? The aim of this ritual is to make the passage into a new state that is as real as the actual world that preceded it in the lives of the new initiates.

Rituals are meticulously put together in ways that suggest the intricacies of technology. The style of a book of liturgical rubrics may not be much different from a manual for building or repairing a complex machine. Even though the form and means are quite different, the principle is the same—how to make actual something that does not exist, but has been created by the human imagination.

Emphasizing freedom and linking it with imagination is worth thinking about.

Robot-boy David's creator, Professor Hobby, tells him that his uniqueness as a robot lies in his ability to enter into the process of self-discovery even though he was not programmed to do so. For David, this process is the quest to become a "real, human boy," replicating the fairy tale of Pinocchio and the search for the Blue Fairy. He was not programmed for this. In fact, Hobby tells him, "we lost you for a few days," precisely because the robot was not expected to embark on such a quest. Alan Turing also accepted this premise in his belief that a thinking machine must learn, search, and make decisions beyond the calculations it was programmed to make, because this is the way human brains operate.

Here we discover one way of defining freedom—behaving in unprogrammed ways (programming, of course, playing the role of determinism). This is a major motif for us today. We are reading this freedom, defined as unprogrammed behavior, into the natural world, in several ways: non-equilibrium thermodynamics, elements of chaos theory, the sciences of "complexity" that incorporate the biochemistry of self-generating processes. The terms "self-generating," "autocatalytic," and "auto-poeisis," are gaining prominence in physics, chemistry, biology, the neurosciences, philosophy, and theology. They refer to the fact that natural processes and things appear, in a way, to "make themselves," in that novelty emerges without direct inter-vention by outside forces. Thinking about "emergence" has focused on this same phenomenon for a hundred years or more in the sciences, philosophy, and theology. Brain scientists speak of the human brain's success in creating novel frame-works or pictures in which it can organize the stimuli it receives from the world in original and significant ways. Scientists have on occasion made this point by say-ing that the human brain succeeds so well because it can supply what is not really there. The function of the imagination is to supply what is not really present in the here and now.

By projecting this freedom into nature, into our physics, chemistry, biology and neurobiology, we are not only taking a giant stride in our way of thinking about nature, we are also abolishing dual-isms, crossing the boundaries between humans and nature, between technology and nature, and between humans and technology. This kind of freedom is what nature and technology and humans share. We could also refer this insight to our image of the techno-mirror. That mirror tells us how important freedom is for us humans. It is so important to us that we strive to create technology that is also free.

Even though breaking down barriers and crossing boundaries is important, what we do after we have crossed the boundaries is even more important. Imagining conditions that are not actual, and believing in them, is one of the most significant things we do when we cross the boundary between humanity and technology, between denying and transcending our actual situation.[3]

Perhaps this imagining is the most important way to define and use our freedom. This freedom is not defined as the lack of restraints, the "don't tread on me" liberty that is so congenial to Americans, particularly to New Englanders. And this freedom is not defined as the license to do and create whatever we wish, the freedom of Prometheus, for example. Rather, this freedom is defined by imagination, the capacity to imagine what is not actual and to take that imagination seriously. Not detective Joe Friday's, "the facts, ma'am, just the facts." Rather, the emphasis is on "what the facts can become." Psychologist Mihaly Csikszentmihalyi believes that it is not possible to live adequately in the world only on the basis of what we know empirically. We also require visions of what the empirical present can become, what its possibilities are. When we envision possibilities, we are in the domain of spirituality. Csikszentmihalyi writes:

> Spiritual values, spiritual ideas, symbols, beliefs and instructions for action point to possibilities which our material nature is not sensitive to. The sensate deals with what is, the spiritual deals with what could be. Spirituality is the focus on the stories and the myths of something more that goes beyond the here and now and tell us what the here and now can become.[4]

Most of the students and practitioners of spirituality that I talk to agree with Csikszentmihalyi's idea.

What I am calling the imagination merges with what Csikszentmihalyi calls the "spiritual." The point is that humans are defined by this imagination or spirituality, freedom is defined by it, and now we see that technology is also defined by this imaginative probing of what actual things and actual states can become—and believing in it, acting on it. That is true spirituality.

Viewed in these terms, technology is a spiritual realm. The question is: What guides the imaginative spirit? I can look out over hundred of acres of forest and imagine that those trees are thousands or millions of board feet of lumber or rolls of newsprint. Or, I can imagine that this is an ecosystem that is home to spotted owls and other diverse species, and that it ought to be cared for as such. Changing the venue, I may look out over the city neighborhood and imagine the unrealized possibilities for development and profit from exploiting the inhabitants. Or I may imagine it as a community of persons, a home for families and individuals, and think of the ways it can be made more wholesome for them all. These differing imagined alternative worlds are equally spiritual, and it makes a difference which world I believe in and commit to.

The imagination must also create larger stories and guiding principles that will direct our beliefs, and these, too, are products of our freedom. We will speak of these in the following chapters.

If imagination is the way we spell freedom and humanness and technology, it is also the way we spell vulnerability. David walked the knife edge of vulnerability in his quest for the Blue Fairy, who he thought could make him what he was not programmed to be. This vulnerability resulted in his imprisonment under the sea in what was formerly Manhattan (Manhattan having been engulfed in the rising seas created by global warming). For two thousand years, David was trapped by a Coney Island Ferris wheel that collapsed on his helicopter as it hovered before a plaster statue of Pinocchio's Blue Fairy—the fairy who could transform David into a real boy. One writer has identified this blue figure with the Virgin Mary. The association is not absurd, since Mary is in some traditions pictured as the epitome of humanity.

His robot friend Gigolo Joe had agonized over David's vulnerability. Professor Hobby agonized as well, because if the robot was open to destruction through this vulnerability, so was his human creator. In *Blade Runner,* the human designers were threatened by their robots' rebellious search for their real humanity. Those designers were murdered by their replicant offspring. In *A.I.,* the vulnerability of the human designer is of a different order. It is not their lives that are threatened so much as the hopes and imagination they have invested in David.

Freedom to be, freedom to imagine, and vulnerability—they go together.

After we emerge from our walking tour within the cyclotron, we recognize this about ourselves, as well. Just as we do when we ponder what our rearranging of biological, genetic matter can become. Whether it is atom bombs or abortions or genetically altered vegetables and human persons, stem cells, embryos, clones— we know ourselves to be both free and vulnerable.

When David, at the end of the movie, lies next to his foster mother and hears her say those magic words, "I love you, David," he knows that he has at last become a real boy. For the first time in his life, he is able to sleep and dream, he has achieved his goal, and in that moment when he falls asleep, he dies—the mortality that belongs to all humans now belongs to him as well. This does not mean that the freedom was bad for him, or demonic. It does not mean that the imagining was the wrong thing to indulge. It does mean that when freedom is really free, and when one is free to imagine things that are not actual—and to believe in them—vulnerability is always part of the mix. It is inherent in the rite of passage into the new that is the future. As Galway Kinnell puts it, "the wages of dying is love."[5]

5

Is Story All There Is?

In his poem, "Thyme Flowering among Rocks," Richard Wilbur describes walking over a field of rocks, in which he says, if it were a Japanese painting, the rocks would represent rough seas where the water "tossed its froth / Straight into the air."[1] But this is not water and foam:

> Here, where things are what
> They are, it is thyme blooming,
> Rocks, and nothing but—

He crouches down to examine the thyme, and finds the complexity of the plant, its stems, its leaves, and its flowers ("fine blue / Or purple trumpets" he calls them). He recognizes that he is "lost now in dense / Fact, fact which one might have thought / Hidden from the sense." He looks so intently at the details of the plant that he loses his sense of the world around him and the plant.

> As, in the motion
> Of striped fins, a bathysphere
> Forgets the ocean.

He closes the poem with these memorable lines:

> It makes the craned head
> Spin. Unfathomed thyme! The world's
> A dream, Basho said,
>
> Not because that dream's
> A falsehood, but because it's
> Truer than it seems.

What I appreciate in this poem is the interaction between the "dense fact" that we find in the things of this world and the idea of dream. The thyme does not and could not exist in utter isolation, in a vacuum; it requires an encompassing world, and yet the plant is so intricate and beautiful that it seems to be a world in and of itself. In its own way, the thyme is "unfathomed." But it does exist in a world.

So, what is the dream? What is the poet suggesting? Is it that we have to separate ourselves from the wider world, dreamlike, before we can notice and appreciate the meticulous detail of the plant? That the plant can become a world of its own only if we dreamily forget everything else? Or is it rather that the facts of the plant are what is real, and the larger world is the dream? It is our dream, our imagination, I will assert, that says the plant is beautiful. It is our imagination that puts the thyme into a tasty dish, an omelet or a fricassee. It is our imagination that decides what that thyme needs to flourish, in our home garden or window box. It is our imagination that will determine whether the field is protected or turned into a shopping mall or upscale condos.

The point is that fact and dream are never separated. The dream, our imagination, does not falsify the fact, but renders it *truer*. Recognizing, of course, that we are the ones who decide what "true" and "truer" mean. The naturalist in the field, the cook in the kitchen, the condo developer, the members of the area zoning committee—all of them think they know what is true. All of them are also working from a basis in dream or imagination, and what they assert about the dense facts of the world is finally inseparable from their dreams. It is even questionable whether any of them would (or could?) make a sharp distinction between fact and dream.

Our reflections on technology have brought us, I believe, to the point where Wilbur was at the end of this poem. Our culture is irretrievably technological. I have suggested that this technology emerges from our freedom to imagine what does not exist and to believe in what is not actual. Our imagination, in turn, takes the form of dreams, narratives, stories about what is not actual. Stories about the possibilities of the actual, to use Csikszentmihalyi's term. Stories about what the present can become.

Alan Turing and his contemporaries would never have even conceived their thinking machines apart from the stories they believed: (1) That logical structure is the essence of the human mind, rather than genes and biology. That's a story, and one with which we might disagree. *A.I.* and *Blade Runner* disagree with one another on this point; *Blade Runner* believes genetics is essential to the reality of mind. (2) That processing information and resolving complex mathematical problems, and cracking Nazi codes were important things for human beings to do. In the process, Turing did create a world of its own, a world so dense, in fact, that it has spawned a community and a culture of experts whose stories are largely inaccessible to most of the people who turn out tasty dishes that depend on the computer technology the experts make possible.

The same can be said of the biotechnologies we have considered. Without the stories that they believed in, James Watson, Francis Crick, and Rosalind Franklin would never have discovered the DNA molecule and the density of its fact would not have been spelled out.

Stories are inseparable not only from the conception of our technology, but also from the uses we imagine for these technologies. It is clear that the two dominant figures in the Human Genome Project, for example, Francis Collins and Craig Venter, worked from powerful stories about who we are and what the goals of life are. Their work with the genome is incomprehensible apart from their stories.

Francis Collins contextualized the genome project in the story of serving humankind and thereby also serving God's purposes. He is a devoted Christian. Craig Venter is equally dedicated, but his story included an essential role for business and the market economy in exploring the possibilities of the genes.

In 1994, *Time* magazine put together an entire issue on the Human Genome Project.[2] It featured two of the then-leading scientists who developed the project: Francis Collins and French Anderson. Collins was photographed in black leather, on his Honda Nighthawk motorcycle. It was the story of *Easy Rider,* the Human Genome Project on the road, in quest of the Holy Grail. Anderson was photographed in his garage, employing tae kwon do techniques to smash a pile of pine boards. This was the story of the Master of Exotic Asian Arts breaking open the mysteries of the genome. Think of the power of these stories and how extraordinary it is that the two scientists were placed within these particular stories. They are highly imaginative constructs, bordering on the mythic, to contextualize the very sensitive technology of the Human Genome Project. It was not the scientists who were telling these stories about themselves. It was society who told these stories—we ourselves. The stories are our ways of contextualizing the technology.

Likewise, there are stories that underlie genetic medicine for therapeutic purposes and others behind the idea of using it to improve individuals and the species. There are stories underlying the pro-life and the pro-choice options for how embryos are handled. There are stories about where life originates, the place of personhood, and the significance of being a living entity.

Such stories are not only inseparable from how we conceive the facts, and how we put them to use, but also for how we justify what we do with them, inseparable from how we decide whether certain uses are desirable or undesirable, good or bad. Let me tell you the story a doctor tells about his work as a clinical geneticist, who frequently performs what is euphemistically called "pregnancy reduction"—terminating one or more fetuses in the womb that are the result of multiple conceptions, which in turn are often the result of fertility therapy. This man is a devout Jew who has wrestled with the issues of his work. He says, "I do evil things. When I am performing my procedures, I am weeping, my patient is weeping, my nurses are weeping. I must do this evil thing, because even greater evil will result if I do not. Quite possibly none of the fetuses will survive birth, and neither will the mother." This story enables him to interpret and justify his use of a certain medical technology. Not everyone will accept his story, but if they don't, they will counter it with an alternative story of their own. Biologist Ursula Goodenough justifies her position on the use of biotechnology for extending the human life span in the context of a story. It is a story of the condition of planet earth at this moment, of population and consumption and the ecological future. Within this story is a story of the human life span and the appropriate attitude toward life and its values. This story contextualizes and justifies her proposal that we not prolong human life indefinitely.[3]

If stories are fused with our experience of the world's fact—whether that fact be thyme or technology—the fact becomes also that we are *dependent* on dream and story. At its most intense, we are dependent upon story for the meaning of technology, or, we might say, of human meaning in a technological culture. We have technology and we have our wider world of nature and human experience. Unless we can put those worlds together, we have no meaning. And without dream, story, and imagination, we cannot put those worlds together. We admire the doctor's and Ursula Goodenough's stories, whether we agree with them or not, because they bring the world of technology and human meaning together.

The tale of Pinocchio and the Blue Fairy drives the reality, in Carlo Collodi's original rendering and also in that of Kubrick and Spielberg. Turing developed meticulous ideas of how machines could simulate humans, but he was also very clear about the distinctions between the two, and his story weaves the similarities and distinctions together. Collodi and the moviemakers tell a story that makes those distinctions very fuzzy, and the fuzziness seems truer today than the sharp distinctions. It is quite appropriate that the forty-first century robots pay tribute to humans, because the existence of the robots depends utterly on the human ability to imagine and to tell the stories that brought robots into being. The robots' words are: "Human beings must be the key of existence. They created millions of meanings of life." These robots embody unambiguously what humans also embody but are often unclear about—that their world and their own existence are dependent on human imagination and story.

In Wilbur's poem, the conclusion that the world's a dream did not emerge from a dreamy state lying on a beach somewhere. It grew out of his close attention to the facts of the physical world. So, too, our insight into the all-pervasive role of imagination and story, our awareness of our dependence upon story—these are not rooted in esoteric theories of academics, and they do not emerge first and foremost from the speculations of French deconstructionist philosophers and literary theorists. They emerge from

Here, where things are what
They are, it is thyme blooming,
Rocks, and nothing but—[4]

It is single-minded attention to the dense facts of technology and our culture of technology that reveals the place of imagination and story. Lynn Randolph did not fantasize about women and machines, she observed and experienced the MRI and the place of women (and men) in today's system of technologized health care. And then she painted her story.

We do not take this news about imagination and story as a matter of course, do we? We are, in fact, quite ambivalent about it. We might even try to kill the messengers who bring the news.

On the one hand, the centrality of imagination and story is exhilarating—that is how Teilhard reacted to it. Story is, after all, something we do so well. Imagining that things can be different, that there can be conditions and worlds alternative to the present is the key to our existence today. In recent congressional hearings on stem cell research, some people testified that alternative worlds are our inalienable right. The father who protested embryo research, on the grounds that the embryo could be preserved and later grow into the charming boy he held in his arms, was insisting on an inalienable right to conditions that differ from the present. The victim of Parkinson's disease, who pleaded that embryo research be approved so that she and others like her could be cured, was arguing the same. Dependence on imagination and story knows no distinction between conservative or liberal, rich or poor, educated or uneducated.

But exhilaration can quickly turn to anger and fear. Most of the people who are known today for their mastery of the dense facts of the world—scientists, engineers, policymakers, and the like—do not cotton to the idea that their work is dependent on imagination and story. Most religious believers share this skepticism about story. Most of the scientists and religious people I know share a dislike for the word *postmodern* precisely because they wish to fence off fact from story. They exhibit anger. I understand that architects and engineers often do not get along very well. The architects suspect that the engineers are bean counters who cannot dream, while the engineers view the architects as dreamers who do not really understand what it takes to construct a building.

There is also fear. To be so free is a fearful thing, because we would like the facts to be immune from our story and imagination. When the doctor tells us that diagnosis is as much an art as a science, our confidence is not strengthened. We would like *our* diagnosis and *our* therapy to be utterly fact-based. We would like the rules governing "is" and "ought" to be rooted in fact, not imagination. That is why "pro-life" and "pro-choice" and pro-and-contra the Kyoto Treaty on global warming are so at odds with each other: they invest their stories with a factuality that cannot tolerate the dimension of imagination. The question about which story is truer is not equivalent to which story is more factual, because we weave the facts and the stories in the same cloth, like warp and weft on a loom.

If our perception of the world is woven from the threads of imagination and story-telling, how we do guard against fooling ourselves, perhaps dangerously? What is the methodology of imagination? What are the criteria for assessing it? How do we determine which dream is truer? These are the key questions: Are there better and worse, more or less adequate, ways of creating and telling our stories? Are there criteria governing our stories? What makes a dream true? These questions are urgent when we reflect on technology.

Wilbur's dream was in close touch with things as "They are, it is thyme blooming, / Rocks and nothing but–." Csikszentmihalyi takes the same tack–spirituality does not contradict empirical reality, but rather proposes what that reality–thyme blooming and rocks–can become. We need large stories to serve this purpose. Recall my earlier example of forests, whether they become lumber, newsprint, or natural conservation areas, or whether neighborhoods become arenas for exploitation or people-friendly communities. What story is truest? What if we include in the story the communities that depend on lumber for their economic welfare, individuals who depend on the jobs that business brings?

Clearly, we have now entered the world of myth and symbol, the world of religion and ritual. In recent years we note proposals to turn the scientific accounts of evolution into an "Evolutionary Epic," serving as the overarching story of the world. Others prefer to extend, revise, and reinterpret traditional creation stories, because they embody time-tested wisdom. Traditional religion may be displaced in some quarters by the modern scientific worldview, but the function of religion to create stories of mythic depth continues to be irreplaceable. The question is, what worldviews can fill this hole left by traditional religion? Would it be either the evolutionary epic or a reinterpreted traditional creation story?

We are looking at the thyme on the rocks as closely as poet Wilbur did, and we are asking, "What *is* the dream? What *is* the story or set of stories that put it all together most adequately and thereby provide human meaning?" At the Parliament of the World's Religions in Cape Town, South Africa, in December 1999, Pinit Ratanakul argued that religion is the place for the examination of these stories.[5] Science is the method for obtaining objectivity concerning external things, whereas Buddhist meditation, for example, is the means for gaining objectivity about internal things, including the imagination and storytelling. At the same symposium, Ursula Goodenough proposed Religious Naturalism, arguing that it is closer to the empirical facts of the world.[6] Speaking from a Hindu perspective, V. V. Raman proposed that science, although it is essential for understanding the world, is not capable of knowing fully the world as humans experience it.[7] For that fuller knowledge, religion is necessary. Such proposals are worthy of our attention. Other religious perspectives would speak of their own contribution to creating and testing the stories.

All of this is integral to the conversation between religion and science—wrestling with the question: When we are confronted with millions of meanings of life, how do we find our way?

6

Cyborgs, Technosapiens,
and God

My plan for this final chapter is straightforward: I will pose two questions for reflection and then elaborate one theological interpretation of technology. The two questions: Where does religion take place? What shape does religion take? My answer: If we speak about technology at its deepest levels, we are at the same time speaking about its religious dimension, even if we do not use conventional religious terminology. All religions that I know believe that human life somehow resonates with the Absolute. For Buddhists, humans can attain enlightenment through disciplined meditational rituals and disengagement from behaviors that cause suffering. Enlightenment is the goal of human existence. Judaism, Christianity, and Islam hold that since humans are created in the image of God, the shape of human existence tends at its deepest level toward God. Saint Augustine embodies this belief in his celebrated prayer: "You have created us for union with yourself, and our hearts are restless until we find our rest in you."[1] Therefore, if we speak clearly and seriously and deeply about humans, we are approaching an understanding of the Absolute. This is where religion happens, at the depth of life. This is where God, or the Absolute, is engaged—at the depths. How do we know that we are at the depth? It is where things make a difference, a life or death difference. It is where we deal with the important things that we do not want to have taken away.[2]

We have painted a picture of ourselves as creatures who integrate in themselves the nature from which we have emerged and the technology that has transformed nature. We have seen that technology is not, most importantly, outside us, but within us, shaping who we are and how we live our lives. *Cyborg* is a relatively recent term that expresses the dimension of techno-nature within human nature. This term originated among NASA scientists who proposed in a technical paper the idea that later surfaced in the movie *Blade Runner,* namely, that instead of creating technology that would enable humans to take a viable environment with them into space, cyborgs should be created who can withstand environments that are hostile to ordinary humans. *Cyborg* refers to creatures that are both organic and technological. *Technosapiens* is a more recent coinage that aims at the same thing.

If the depth dimension is *where* religion—or we could say, spirituality—happens, then techno-human, cyborg, and technosapiens are terms that describe the *form* or shape of religion. This is a difficult saying, because our conventional ideas about religion give it any shape except technology. Pretechnological, simple, pastoral, isolated, untouched—even rural, as well as spectacular landscapes and fierce elements, wind and sea—these are more likely to be associated with religion and the holy, in both traditional and more revisionist perspectives.

Some years ago, my denomination polled its members on the question, "If you have had a religious experience or an experience of God, where did it happen?" Sixty-five percent of the responses of those who had such experiences reported that they happened in a church service, while the rest happened in a beautiful or impressive landscape, like the Rocky Mountains or the Grand Canyon. In other words, the religious experiences were associated with designated holy places or with the awesome aspects of nature.

If we hold to this conventional view of religion, it means that the shape of this religion has very little explicitly to do with technology. You can see the problem immediately: if, on the one hand, technology is the arena in which some of the most important things are happening to human nature, if technology is the medium for new selves and new identities to emerge, as Teilhard suggests, and, on the other hand, we cannot imagine that religion takes shape in technology, then we have eliminated the religious or depth dimension of the most significant developments in human becoming. This is a dangerous development. To banish the depth dimension from technology leaves us very vulnerable.

Is this an anthropocentric or human-centered reading? Of course it is. But there is a new element here. Now that we have broken down the walls that separate humans from both nature and technology, now that we are crossing the boundaries between these domains, we see that humans and their technology are a set of nature's possibilities. Humans are not what they used to be, so anthropocentrism is not the same, either. The religion of cyborgs and technosapiens, therefore, is also a religion of nature. If we speak in Jewish-Christian-Muslim terms, we must say that technonature is creation and cyborg is created in the image of God. If we subscribe to Religious Naturalism, we will have to say that technology is as much a dimension of the natural as the sea, the landscape, the biosphere, and other elements of the evolutionary process. Technology is now a phase of evolution, and it is now creation, a vessel for the image of God.

We have come to see that the very existence of technology rests upon the inherent freedom and capacity for imagination that marks human being. Finally we have seen how we not only create worlds in our technology that do not yet exist, but we also create the meaning and justification and purpose of those worlds. We not only create the worlds, but we also must create the ideas of right and wrong that are required if those worlds are to be wholesome. Not only do we create the technology that the clinical geneticist uses, and not only the human techniques that alter the environment of the mother's womb, but we also create the meanings and justifications of it all. I have tried to capture this dimension of human nature by speaking of us as *created cocreators*. I believe that such an idea is a basis for interpreting technology generally, but also religiously and theologically.

If we are to speak of religion, it must be religion that can encompass the human life that is cyborg and technosapiens. It cannot be merely a religious way of *dealing* with technology, as if technology was external to who we are. It must be a possibility for the religion of the cyborgs, a possibility for us who are now the techno-humans.

We must ask ourselves, what is liturgy, what is sacrament for the cyborg? What is our theology of nature in the light of our own nature as techno-nature? What is our ecological ethic toward techno-nature?

What do the terms "pro-life" and "pro-choice" mean in the age of "techno-life"? Such questions now come to center stage. We see even now that the technology of embryo research is rearranging the lines and the strategies of what we call "pro-choice" and "pro-life."

What of the Absolute? What do we say about God in this techno-world? If, as the religions believe, human life resonates to the Absolute, what can we say about this resonance? Let me present six questions that I have formulated as I have contemplated the issues that have emerged.

1. God is a *participant* in the technological process, since the purposes of God are now embodied through technology and techno-nature. How do we understand God's technological purposes?

2. If the techno-human, the cyborg, is created in the image of God, what does that tell us about God?

3. If God not only desires freedom and imagination, but intends nature, in its human and subsequent forms, to be free and free to imagine what is not yet actual, and to commit its life to what

can be imagined, what does this tell us about the nature and will of God?

4. If God prefers not to tell us what things mean, but rather for us to create the meanings and discover which are most viable, if God has created a nature which is dependent upon imagination and story, what does that tell us about the nature of God and the nature of the creation? If we are created with the inherent mandate to transcend ourselves, what can we conclude about God? What can we conclude about the goal and fulfillment of the creation?

5. What can we say about a God who seems more inclined to ask us who we are, rather than to tell us who we are?

6. What is the significance of the fact that on our planet, at least, God has set up a system in which the creatures who transcend humans in the chain of evolution may be creatures we have designed and created, so that their act of transcending us is at the same time our own act of transcending ourselves?

These questions are as yet unanswered. They are the theological questions of the era of techno-nature, the theological questions asked by cyborg. They are the questions for which we are the theologians.

I am not going to deal with these questions in detail. Rather, I will propose one set of theological reflections that may throw light on all of the questions.

If self-generation, autopoeisis–the making of ourselves–is written into the very substance of nature, as well as into the fundamental code of human nature and technology, we must consider that it is a clue to the nature of reality and, therefore, to the nature of God. The same is to be said about the apparent fact that we are not given the meanings of nature and human life–not by nature nor by God–but apparently we have to discern meaning, create it, and we must decide what is more true or less true about our own creations. This is also a clue to the nature of reality. Finally, the fact that rearranging matter, supercreating, and bringing new possibilities into existence are basic to human nature–this, too, is a clue to the nature of God.

Let me take a moment, following the trail of these clues, to say where I see God in the movies *Blade Runner* and *A.I.* One of the leading motifs in these movies is that the robots' drive to transcend themselves must be acknowledged. Neither movie will allow it to be ignored or dismissed. This is a matter of urgency in both movies—it drives the plots, it creates tension, it is troubling, both to the movies' characters and to the audience. The robots simply cannot abandon their quest, whether it is a quest for reengineering, as in *Blade Runner,* or the Pinocchio quest to be transformed by love, as in *A.I.*

One of the classical assertions about God in traditional religions is that God speaks the difficult word that puts people on the pressure point of life; God will not let them off, and forces them to deal with hard reality. In *Blade Runner* and *A.I.,* both the human designers and the robots are kept on that pressure point. In *Blade Runner,* the designers are not allowed to escape their own incompetence and the drive of their replicants for fuller human existence. The designers die at the hands of the robots. But the robots, as well, are forced to deal with their reality, and we see that the male replicant, Roy, must succumb to his mortality, with self-awareness and dignity, and although Rachel is fully aware of her situation as a replicant, we are left uncertain about her resolution of her mortality. Spielberg has been criticized for not ending *A.I.* at an earlier point in the narrative. However, an earlier ending would have let the characters off the hook. David must complete his quest and experience the mortality that goes with it. I see the presence of God in both films, in this pressure for the characters to fulfill the drive toward their humanity, whether it is successful or not. By pursuing it, they are successful. The human designers and the robots are caught up in self-transcending creativity and the presence of God will not let them abandon it.

Classically, God is also the One who speaks the word of possibility to the creation and sustains its drive toward that possibility. I see this, too, in both movies, even though neither has a conventional "happy ending." What does this assert about religious depth and the possible action of God? I suggest that it puts the focus on the phenomenon of transcendence. Earlier, I observed that transcendence is a fundamental element of both human nature and technology—transcendence in the sense of imagining and believing and cocreating what is not actual, and creating the meaning of what is imagined, as well.

At its depth, reality *is* a process constituted by this drive for transcending. *Exploration of possibilities that are not yet actual is the nature of reality.* Is nature enough? Of course it is. But nature is never satisfied with itself; it always presses to be more and it presses for novelty. When we participate in this drive for new possibilities, we participate also in God. This is the dimension of holiness in technology. The difference between a nontheological and a theological interpretation of technology is that the one says the transcending drive is epiphenomenal, a surface phenomenon, while theology says it is rooted in the very nature of things. The epiphenomenalist says that the transcending is evolution's way of promoting fitness. The theologian asserts rather that evolution has itself been designed to enable a self-transcending system of reality.

When we are immersed in the drive for transcendence, are we thereby sharing in the ultimate depths of reality that we can call God? Or are we participating in a process of selection and advance that is finally without meaning? Is the fire of our lives a match struck for a few moments, only to sputter as it goes out? Or is it part of a larger flame that underlies all reality and that has eternal meaning? *This is, at its heart, the religious question, and it points to the religious dimension of technology.*

The profound, and perhaps ironic, fact here is that we must discover whether there is deeper meaning to the struggle for transcendence, and we must construct and create that meaning. If the meaning were given to us, like tablets of gold buried in the earth or tablets of stone brought down from the mountaintop, it would mean that final meaning does not require our self-transcending act of creation. It would mean that, at its depth, reality is not a self-transcending mystery, but a set of prearranged meanings and truths. The very fact that the world appears to be random and void of meaning unless we create the meaning leaves open the possibility that self-transcending itself is an ultimate reality. Reality is this self-transcending freedom to imagine and to believe in what is imagined. This is reality, "thyme blooming / Rocks, and nothing but—"—all the way down. There are never any tablets of gold to be found.

This is the leap of faith, to wager that the search for meaning is in fact the meaning. God has created us for this, to create meaning in freedom with no deterministic programming to do so. Recall Augustine's words, in his *Confessions*: "You have created us for union with yourself, and our hearts are restless until we find our rest in you." Union may be the goal, union with meaning, union with God, but restlessness is the medium. Restlessness is as fundamental as meaning, because restlessness is the meaning. Our drive for self-transcendence is an expression of this restlessness. Technology is therefore also an expression of it. We encounter God, share in God, through that restlessness. In my tradition, we could say that technological restlessness is a means of grace. We ascribe the term to the bread and wine of Holy Communion, the water of Baptism, as well as to the community and its relationships of mutual support and love, because these can be vehicles of God's love. By analogy, we must also see the appropriateness of interpreting technological restlessness as a means of grace.

Did the replicants in *Blade Runner* fail? Was their struggle wasted? Must we say the same about their fallible and incompetent designers? Was robot-boy David's dying a sign of defeat for him and his designer? And what about his foster mother, Monica? Or did they all find in their struggle and dying their access to depth and ultimacy? Union with God? Their dying marked the end of their portion of the self-transcending struggle, but it underscored their commitment to final meaning. It underscored that they placed love for God, the source and power of self-transcendence, above all else. They would not give up. It marked their union with God, not their alienation.

This is not the whole of the human story, nor the whole of the religious story. I believe, however, that it is a piece of that meaning and a fragment of the religious meaning of technology. Technology is either pointless in the long run, or it is an expression of the fundamental self-transcending reality of God.

I close with a set of proposals:

Technology is itself a sacred space.

Technology is itself a medium of divine action, because technology is about the freedom of imagination that constitutes our self-transcendence.

Technology is one of the major places today where religion happens. Technology is the shape of religion, the shape of the cyborg's engagement with God.

Since we are cyborgs, technology is also the place where, like Jacob, we wrestle with the God who comes to engage us.

Epilogue

Interpreting Technology through Visual Metaphor

Lynn Randolph's painting *La Mestiza Cosmica* embodies the concerns that underlie this book. For this reason, I have placed it at the very beginning, as frontispiece. Randolph writes of her work:

In a society that increasingly is dependent upon the link between cognition and seeing through amazing new imaging technologies, I want to create images that trouble, resist, and disturb and offer provisional visions of love, hope, and well-being. . . . I'm trying to create metaphors that chart new ways of thinking and change the symbolic order. Visual metaphors call upon the beholder to combine and synthesize experiences that [are] fragmented or dissected.[1]

Creating metaphors "that chart new ways of thinking and change the symbolic order" is precisely what I consider to be the central task of theology today, and it is what I have attempted in this book. Randolph's is a more difficult and more powerful medium, but the task demands that we approach it in as many forms and media as possible.

La Mestiza Cosmica epitomizes the search for the human meaning of technology. Even though its richness in combining and synthesizing fragmented experiences defies written description, I will attempt it here. The central figure is a *mestiza,* a woman of "mixed" (from the word *mestizaje*) heritage, representing both literal and symbolic "mixing." Alex Garcia-Rivera defines *mestizaje* as "the process of biological and cultural mixing that occurs after the violent and unequal encounter between cultures. . . . [it] also creates frontiers."[2] Traditionally, in Mexican history, this "mixing" referred to the Spanish, African, and Indian parentage—biological and cultural. The Mestiza retrieves Mary in the tradition of the Virgin of Guadalupe, who in her appearance in 1531 to Juan Diego, a Mexican Indian, symbolizes God's redemptive presence among the poorest segments of Mexican society. She is still a vivid presence for liberation among Mexicans on both sides of the Rio Grande river. Our Lady of Guadalupe does not represent Mary as a mother, but rather relates her to the Virgin of the Apocalypse. Thus, in her very portrayal, she speaks of both the gift and the threat of technology for human existence.

The woman stands astride the Rio Grande River (the artist is a Texan, living in Houston), which itself is a frontier between the "mixed" cultures of Mexico and the United States. Virgilio Elizondo speaks of this Rio Grande area as the "frontier zone of a new human race," those who are thoroughly "mixed" in several dimensions of life.[3]

This Mary does not crush the serpent, she tames it (its rattlesnake markings resemble those of a DNA representation) in one hand, as she manipulates the Hubble Space Telescope in the other (recalling also that NASA is headquartered in the Houston area). The four hands suggest the Aztec goddess Coatlicue. She surmounts the planet, against the background of our galaxy and the moon. She is at once a

Christian religious symbol, representing the liberation of an oppressed population and its pre-Christian heritage, and also at home in the world of science and technology, bending them to her larger purposes in a cosmic context. And she represents the human race that is becoming new, in the person of a woman.

This Cosmic Mestiza does not ratify the past or the present that she so vividly portrays. Rather, she synthesizes them in a vision of the future that is neither soft nor easy. She knows well that this future has a sinister face as well as a promising lure. In her person she both honors and rejects the past and present. She creates frontiers, charts new ways of thinking, and points to new possibilities for love, hope, and well-being. In opening up a new range of symbols, Lynn Randolph speaks of her paintings as "hypertexts," "interactively readable; not finally fact or statement, but metaphors for a provisional reality that I hope will connect to the realities of others."[4] As hypertext, the Cosmic Mestiza is a metaphor for human becoming in the medium of a technologized world. As such, she symbolizes the restless struggle that marks every page of this book.

Notes

1. Locating the Spiritual Journey

1. Wallace Stevens, "Anecdote of the Jar," in *The Collected Poems of Wallace Stevens* (New York: Vintage, 1990), 76. Used by permission.

2. Pierre Teilhard de Chardin, "Some Reflections on the Spiritual Repercussions of the Atom Bomb," in *The Future of Man*, ed. Norman Denny (London: Collins, 1964), 141.

3. Teilhard, "On Looking at a Cyclotron," in *Activation of Energy*, ed. René Hague (New York: Harcourt Brace and Jovanovich, 1971), 351.

4. Teilhard, *Future of Man*, 144.

5. Teilhard, *Activation of Energy*, 352.

6. Teilhard, *Future of Man*, 145.

2. The Movement from Techno-World to Techno-Self

1. A. O. Scott, "Do Androids Long for Mom?" *New York Times*, 29 June 2001, B8.

2. Donna J. Haraway, *Modest_Witness@ Second_Millennium. FemaleMan_Meets_Onco-Mouse: Feminism and Technoscience* (New York: Routledge, 1997), xiii–xiv. Emphasis added.

3. Joseph Dumit, "Mindful Images: PET Scans and Personhood in Biomedical America" (Ph.D. diss., University of California at Santa Cruz, 1995), 86.

3. Seeing Ourselves in the Techno-Mirror

1. Andrew Hodges, *Alan Turing: The Enigma* (New York: Simon and Schuster, 1983), 415.

2. Ibid., 406, 413.

3. Ibid., 292.

4. Ibid., 219.

5. Frank J. Tipler, *The Physics of Immortality: Modern Cosmology, God, and the Resurrection of the Dead* (New York: Anchor, 1994).

6. These comments are based on the "director's cut" of *Blade Runner,* which differs from the "theater" version, which imposed a happy ending on the movie.

7. Paul Tillich, *Systematic Theology,* vol. 1. (Chicago: University of Chicago Press, 1951), 14.

8. Ernest Becker, *The Denial of Death* (New York: Free Press, 1973).

4. The Essence

1. Pierre Teilhard de Chardin, "Some Reflections on the Spiritual Repercussions of the Atom

Bomb," in *The Future of Man*, ed. Norman Denny (London: Collins, 1964), 144.

2. Ibid., 146.

3. See Donna Haraway's descriptions of boundaries and boundary-crossing in the context of technology in *Simians, Cyborgs, and Women: The Reinvention of Nature* (New York: Routledge, 1991), 149–82, 203–30.

4. Mihaly Csikszentmihalyi, "Consciousness for the Twenty-First Century," *Zygon: Journal of Religion and Science* 26 (March 1991): 23.

5. Galway Kinnell, "Little Sleep's-Head Sprouting Hair in the Moonlight," *The Book of Nightmares* (New York: Houghton-Mifflin, 1971), 53.

5. Is Story All There Is?

1. These and the following lines are from Richard Wilbur, "Thyme Flowering among Rocks," in *Walking to Sleep: New and Collected Poems* (New York: Harcourt Brace and Jovanovich, 1988), 142–43. Used by permission.

2. Special issue on the Human Genome Project, *Time*, January 17, 1994.

3. Goodenough's comments are from her unpublished paper, "Biotechnology and the Length of Life," delivered at the Star Island Conference, 2001.

4. Wilbur, "Thyme Flowering among Rocks," 142.

5. Pinit Ratanakul, "Buddhism and Science: Allies or Enemies?" *Zygon* 37 (March 2002): 115–20.

6. Ursula Goodenough, *The Sacred Depths of Nature* (New York: Oxford University Press, 1998), xvii–xviii, and passim.

7. V. V. Raman, "Science and Spiritual Vision: A Hindu Perspective," *Zygon* 37 (March 2002), 83–94.

6. Cyborgs, Technosapiens, and God

1. 2. *Augustine: Confessions and Enchiridion*, ed. Albert C. Outler (Philadelphia: Westminster Press, 1955).

2. See Paul Tillich, "The Lost Dimension in Religion," in *The Spiritual Situation in Our Technical Society*, ed. J. Mark Thomas (Macon, Ga.: Mercer University Press, 1988), 41–48.

Epilogue

1. Lynn Randolph, "Cyborgs, Wonder Woman, and Techno-Angels: A Series of Spectacles," an unpublished paper presented on 23 April 1996 at the Center for the Critical Analysis of Contemporary Culture, Rutgers University, 1–3. See also her website: www.lynnrandolph.com.

2. Alex Garcia-Rivera, *St. Martin de Porres: The "Little Stories" and the Semiotics of Culture* (Maryknoll, N.Y.: Orbis Books, 1995), 40.

3. Virgilio Elizondo, *The Future Is Mestizo: Life Where Cultures Meet* (Bloomington, Ind.: Meyer-Stone Books, 1988), x.

4. Randolph, "Cyborgs," 15.